HEALING MAMA

Written by **Amanda Nube**, Illustrated by **Lynn Gottlieb**

On the day I was born the angels sang, the gods danced, the earth shook. Mama cried out, "Bring her to me!" And the doctors cried out, "Bring her to me." And so they did. Mama cried and I cried. Papa sang and I sang.

When I found Mama's breast again I drank, and I drank, and I drank. Mama sang, Mama stared, and Mama snoozed. I knew then that we are each born with a gift and a challenge: Mine is both - Healing Mama.

For my first birthday Mama took me Outside. The moon shone bright through the dark night sky. Mama sang, "Luna, Luna Llena. Luna, Luna Bella. Moon, Full Moon. Moon, Beautiful Moon. Moon of Love, Moon of Life. Gift us your guidance. Gift us your light."

Each year, one more cycle was completed around the sun. Each year, Mama would take me out under the full moon and sing that song. I made up my own songs too. I even sang to the moon when she was not bright or I could not see her.

One night, close to the time of my 13th cycle around the sun, I went Outside. I felt compelled. I knew the Dark Moon was there. I felt sad. I sang a silent song in my heart and walked a ways. I stopped and stood in silence. I listened. "Bring her to me," said my Abuela Moon. "Bring her to me," said Grandmother Moon.

And so it was decided, Mama and I would go to her. We slept well for the next 13 nights preparing for our journey. When the moon shone bright through the dark night sky we went Outside. We were not alone. Everywhere we looked there were mothers, new and old, standing with their faces turned towards the fullness of the moon. We turned our faces to the moon and sang our song, Luna Bella. Then we stood in silence and waited, listening, listening to the silence.

And the Moon said: "Welcome Mama. Welcome Daughter. I have been waiting. I have watched you, watching me, and I will watch over you now as you step out onto new ground. You are not alone. Look around and you will see many faces of all different hues yet not unlike your own. Faces mourning the mothers they left behind or never had. Faces looking into the faces of the unborn and the new born, wondering, will they be able to give what they have not received? Faces that eventually turn to me and plead: Mama Moon, please take these burdens from me, I can't take them any more. It gets so dark, too dark to see. 'Imeinu Mokoreinu,' they sing. 'Our Supreme Mother,' in every tongue they sing. Go now. Return to who you are, return to what you are, return to the land of your soul." "Where?" we ask. "There is a tree. She is a tree of life. Lost souls look to her. Found souls thank her for all life that comes from her roots. Remove your shoes, the ground you walk upon is holy. Feel it."

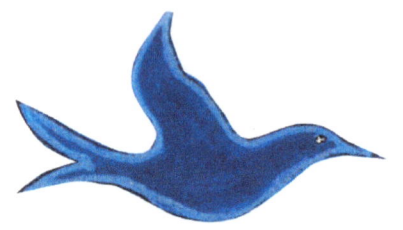

Holy ground under bare feet?

That was not easy for Mama. She hated getting dirty. She never took her shoes off. She even wore socks to bed! The ground was covered in shards of sharp twigs and rocks. Mama found a nearby stump and sat down to rest. We looked around, it was dark. We could not decide which tree Grandmother Moon was talking about.

"Perhaps this stump was the tree." Mama said. "It looks old. It looks like it was important. Too bad it was cut down. These days no one goes to the 'Tree of Life,' walks on 'Holy Ground,' or acknowledges our 'Roots'. These are old words from an old world. Money does not grow on trees. We have to work. We have to put food on our table. I don't think we should be out anymore. It's not safe. It's not smart. I'm sorry. We tried, but it is no use." Mama's head and heart looked heavy. She pulled her coat tight around her and shivered. We put on our shoes and walked home.

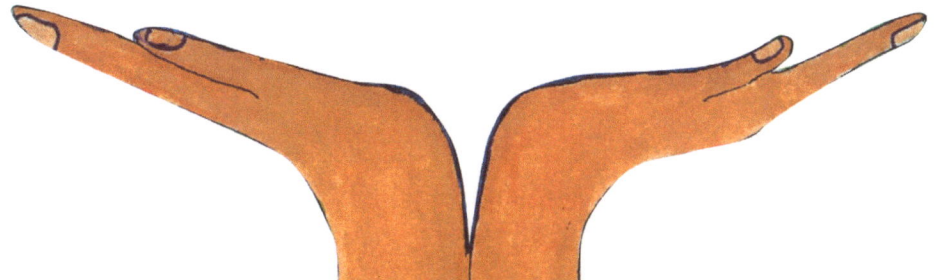

That night I had a dream: I walked out of our house into the most beautiful garden in the light of day. Mama was there trimming roses. She was happy. I saw a tree stump in the center of the garden and went over to it. I sat down. As I looked down I could see well below the surface of the earth. I saw Mama there too. She held out a seed and handed it to me. I put the seed in my mouth and ate it. I looked down at my feet and saw that from them great roots grew. The stump started to grow too, it grew branches all around me. A beautiful weave of branches surrounded me and formed a great basket. I was right in the middle. I looked up and saw a circular clearing. Through the clearing I could see to the stars. Through the stars I saw a constellation. It was a woman, holding a bowl of fruit.

"I want to go out this morning." I announced when I awoke. "Outside. To find Life or the Tree of Life or Something. There's got to be more to life than this." Mama agreed. She put on her shoes, then took them off again, remembering what Grandmother Moon had instructed. And so we walked, and we sang, and we stopped. We had never seen such bright colors, heard so many birds and insects, smelled such an array of fragrances. Mama let me climb and embrace many of the trees we found. "Are you the Tree? The Tree of Life?" I asked while up in the branches. "Yes!" Each one said so. "Mama, This is it!" "No, it's this one!" Mama had also heard a "Yes" from the tree she lay down under. "Oh," we decided, "THEY ARE ALL HOLY!" Every tree, every bee, every flower, every worm.

Many days were happily spent in those gardens. Soon the time came to return again to Grandmother Moon shining bright in the early night sky.

And the Moon said: "Ah, Yes. Holy is the silence, holy is the sound, holy is each one of us, and holy is the ground. You have learned well dear ones. Like the owl, your sight is brighter. Like the doe, your ears attuned. Your smell is keener and your belly fuller. The skin on your feet free. You are more alive, your bodies like the tree of life, bearing fruit, roots, and branches. Now it is time for you to learn the ocean's song. Watch the turning of her tides as you watch your own tides. Tune in to the body."

We thanked Grandmother Moon and

walked home. The next day Mama was busy, she decided to get a tune-up. She had not been taking care of her body as much as she had been taking care of mine. She went to see Dr. Grey. He did some tests. She went to see Dr Chiro. He said Mama could use some meditation. She went to see a guru. He did not speak, but taught Mama how to breathe. Every morning she would get up early to breathe. But there were dark circles under her eyes.

One night, when the moon was dark in the night sky, I went outside. "Moon," I asked, "Where are you? Even in darkness, I know you are there. Mama sits in darkness too. Is she in tune with her body now?" No answer.

In the days to come Mama grew more tired. She didn't go to classes or doctors. She stayed home taking long baths. She opened the windows and left them open, night after night. She stared out the window, listening to the ocean.

One night, she went Outside. She walked down to the ocean. I watched her from the window. Her body swayed in rhythms I had not seen before. She cried. I did not disturb her. She stayed there a long time, watching the tide come in and the tide roll out. Each night, the moon grew brighter as did Mama, until it was full again, time to return again.

Mama knelt, Mama wept, and Mama spoke: "Luna, Luna Llena. Moon, Full and Beautiful Moon. Thank you. Thank you Great Moon above. Thank you for showing me your ways, your faces, your rhythms. I have followed you across the sky, chasing the sun. I too found myself chasing doctors and gurus and performing sun salutations. But when I looked within I saw my own dark side and light side, just like you. I have cycles within me too throughout the month. Thank you for teaching me how to honor these phases in my body as I honor these phases of yours. Please continue to gift me your wisdom so that I may also give these gifts to my daughter."

And the Moon said: "Se abre el cuerpo, se abren las emociones - When the body opens, the emotions open. I am so pleased that you learned to listen and watch your own body's wisdom and rhythms. And now you must listen to the words of the wind. Whispers passed down through the generations. You know them well enough. They have called you here to me. Some are not mild winds, nor do they carry mere words. There are wounds. Tread carefully. Look down the long line. They are there waiting."

And so we wound our way down,

down, down, to the place where all souls rest. There we saw an elaborate labyrinth of stone and brush. Mama entered. I stayed at the entrance, standing guard. For what? I didn't know.

I watched as Mama walked down the first path. Her form grew smaller and smaller, younger and younger. She continued down the winding paths. Sometimes nearer, sometimes farther. Sometimes skipping, sometimes pausing. There were objects along the way, memories from her past, voices and whispers on the wind. "Céad Míle Fáilte!" The ancestors called out. "A Hundred Thousand Welcomes." As she approached the center, I strained to see her, so far down the line was she. And she was not alone. Her own mother was there to receive her.

Mama fell to her knees and picked up an old doll. She cradled the doll in her arms a long time, sobbing. Then she looked up at the vision of her own distant mother. She saw the look of an anguished mother, restrained even as she gave birth. She saw the mother that did not hold or swaddle her child as a babe. The mother that never uttered a kind word or placed a tender kiss on her young temples. She saw her mother's hidden anguish, blame, shame, and rage. Then Mama looked up at the Moon, still watching over us as ever.

"This is not my pain." Mama declared. "It is my mother's pain, and perhaps even her mother's before her. Please take it from her. Take it from them. Take it from me. I can't carry it any more. Its not mine. It's not my pain. It's her pain. Oh Moon, Dear Moon..." She went on, "She is in so much pain. I am so sorry for her. I loved her so much. I locked up that pain and threw away the key, as had she. But I felt the cold. I felt the bitterness. I felt the sorrow. Mostly, I felt numb. Only from time to time could I feel love."

Mama looked back down at the doll, still cradling her. "Its OK," She murmured. "It's OK to cry and feel and love and open. No one will hurt you. I'm here now. I love you. I love you with all the love that was meant for me and the love that is meant for my daughter." With that, Mama stood. She stood tall and broad and a radiance shone from behind her. She returned from the center of the wind labyrinth to the entrance where I awaited her return. She hugged and kissed me emphatically.

And the Moon said: "Now I turn to you, Daughter. Will you open to me as I open to you." "Yes," I said. "You sing your own songs, and your journey is your own. You opened your mother's heart on the day you were born and helped her to sing the songs within her. You have listened well all these years. You have listened with your heart and you have listened to your heart. Now, my daughter, your belly will warm and your heart will soar. This is the joining of body and fire. Follow your feet. Father Sun will watch over you."

Mama followed me. "I too have so much to learn. I never made this journey with my own mother. But I make it now," she said.

I felt a knot in my belly and watched as the moon dipped and the sun rose. And rose. And rose. We walked, Mama and I. We walked but did not see the way. We could not sing, our voices dry. The sun shone bright, we shielded our eyes and followed our feet. The sand was hot below. We looked for shelter from the heat and stopped to lay waiting for evening to come. I lay face down, belly down. I let the heat spread over my body and take me to the center of the liquid earth. I felt a warmth trickling down my legs. It was blood.

"Mama!" I cried. "Oh," she said, as the blood turned into rays of rainbow light against my skin, then transformed into a river of rainbow serpents as they slithered across the sand. She came to me and touched my feet. She began to massage my feet and legs with her hands. My body felt at once tight and painful as well as soft and comforted. She massaged every inch of me as I drifted through time and space in dreams. I imagined Mama and I riding the river of rainbow serpents to a great big fire where there was music and dancing.

When I opened my eyes some time later I could still hear the drumming. Now it was night. Mama was there, still massaging and soothing me. No serpents, but a rainbow tattoo appeared around my left ankle. "Do you hear that?" asked Mama. "Yes." I said, "It's a party."

We followed the music, followed the rhythms, the drums, the voices, the sounds of hands clapping and feet dancing. We saw a bright fire blazing and the shapes of women, perhaps wild, dancing, drumming, singing, swaying. Many of their bodies were bare, adorned only with paint and handmade jewelry. Some wore long skirts. Some had tattoos like the rainbow around my ankle. Some had tattoos of black serpents, red moons, or yellow lightning bolts. A group of girls my age ran up to greet us. They took my hand and guided me to a special place. A group of women fussed over me, brushing and braiding my hair, anointing my body with oils, and offering me fresh fruit.

"Come," the women and girls said. We followed them into the Red Tent. They taught us their fire songs. I asked what the tattoos meant and one by one they told their stories. The dark serpent, in honor of the dark moods that took over some months. The red moon, in honor of the great force of blood that makes walking and working impossible some days. The yellow lightning, in honor of the healing visions beneath the flashing pains that used to blind some. They spoke of their struggles with these "gifts" which also led them to seek the moon's counsel and each others' console.

"And the rainbow?" I asked. "Ah, the rainbow gift," said the woman who sat closest to Mama, "is the gift of creative fire. It can be beautiful, but it can also be elusive. All these gifts are ours to master. Many will never see them, never find their unique gift along with their menses. Many will only recall their pain and moods as a curse and not a blessing. We are the ones who have learned to say 'Thank You' to our Grandmother Moon, to ask for her guidance, and to carry on her teachings."

"Thank you," I said, not really knowing what it all meant. We laughed and went out to dance under the waning moonlight, hands and hearts joined in sweet connection with our sisters. So grateful, so graceful. We stayed for days. We were given a place to sleep and a role to play in this sacred gathering. Then as the moon turned to hide again in darkness, each packed up and said her goodbyes. "We meet. We part. And we will meet again!" They chimed.

Everything seemed different and exactly the same when we arrived home. Mama said I was a woman now, though I still thought of myself as a girl. "Keep it that way, my child." Mama said. "I too have felt like a girl these nights and it has felt SO good. I have never laughed so hard!" She stretched her arms out wide and gave me a hug.

We rested many nights. We walked down the way during the day. I met new friends who lived nearby. As the moon grew fuller again I wondered what would await us this time? What now? I recalled a song my friends of the red tent had sung, we had sung. And I sang, "The river is flowing, flowing and growing. The river is flowing back to the sea. Oh Mother carry me, your child I will always be, Oh Mother carry me, back to the sea." I sang as we headed out to our special place, awaiting the rise of our beloved teacher on the eastern horizon.

FIRST MOON'S TEACHINGS:

The ground we walk on is sacred. Nature opens our senses and connects our bodies to the body of Earth. Through her daughter's persuasion, Mama opens up to experience the great outdoors, the magic of nature, and the awakening of her senses. The voice of the moon here references several key concepts from Hebrew liturgy, albeit feminized. "Imeinu Mokoreinu," translated as "Our Supreme Mother," is an adaptation of the song and the plea of "Avinu Malkeinu," or "Our Supreme Father." "Return to who you are…Return to the land of your soul" is sung at the time of the Hebrew lunar calendar's new year, a time to practice "T'shuva" which means repair & return. "Holy is the silence… And holy is the ground" is also a modern and feminized Jewish hymn by Taya Shere taken from Siddur HaKohanot.

SECOND MOON'S TEACHINGS:

Ocean tides, tears, and water in general, carry and cleanse the emotions of the soul. Mama learns to tune into her body and her emotions, first with the help of outside guides, and ultimately by following her own inner compass. The voice of the moon here references the wise words of Estela Roman, from Nuestra Medicina: Indigenous Medicine of Mexico. "Se abre el cuerpo, se abren las emociones," translates as 'When the body opens, the emotions open." Spiritual teachers, therapists, and healers across many traditions reveal that our physiology affects our psychology, and vice versa. When we tend to the body we make room for tending to the hidden undercurrents of the emotions.

THIRD MOON'S TEACHINGS:

Putting on airs means to behave in a way that isn't true. Voices from our past are like air, carrying words and messages passed down through the generations. Through facing, feeling, and releasing our ancestor's words and our ancestor's wounds, we enable our lineage to not repeat old cycles. We can foster new growth so that the next generation can inherit a legacy healed, not at war with itself. Mama learns to forgive the wounds passed down to her from her foremothers and forefathers.

FOURTH MOON'S TEACHINGS:

It is said that the moon is especially close to women because she governs the natural cycle of menstruation. This cycle is a gift to women. It is a powerful time of cleansing mentally, physically, emotionally and spiritually. Mama and Daughter stay close to each other as Daughter embarks on her own initiation into womanhood and community with the onset of her first menstrual cycle. In many traditions, when a young woman had her first menstruation her female relatives would celebrate with her and she would be given teachings about the power of women. Today, many modern families are returning to these traditions and are reviving the practices of the Moon Lodge or Red Tent. The song, "The river is flowing…." is a popular folk song that I learned at various women's gatherings. One such gathering is the Northern California Women's Herbal Symposium, where my daughter and I first experienced a similar rite of passage, fire circle, and red tent, to the one I wrote about. Fire connects us to creativity and it connects us to our customs and celebrations as a human community.

GRATITUDE

Thank you to the worlds and elements of Assiah, Yetzirah, Briah, and Atziluth. Thank you to my mother and father, my sister and brother, and all my grandparents. Thank you to Mateo Nube, Nilo Nube, & Barbara Nube. Thank you to Lynn Gottlieb for the beautiful artwork and Innosanto Nagara for the expertise, design, and guidance. Thank you to all those who supported my book creation & launch campaign; Shoshana Uribe, Julia Katz, Rebecca Redstone, Nomy Lamm, Sarah Tzipurah Moser, Gail Koffman, Jennifer Griffin, Indelisa Carillo, Marni Rothman, Todd Stuart, Rebecca Elswit, Erin MacDonnell, Nicole Farkouh, Sheryl Alder Eldridge, Leiah Borrowsky, and Dawn Holman. And immense gratitude and appreciation to Maya Zahar Nube, my daughter, my bright and guiding light.

For information on retreats, camps, rites of passage ceremonies, and circles for women and daughters, contact me at Amanda@HealingMama.com. I welcome your inquiry and journey.

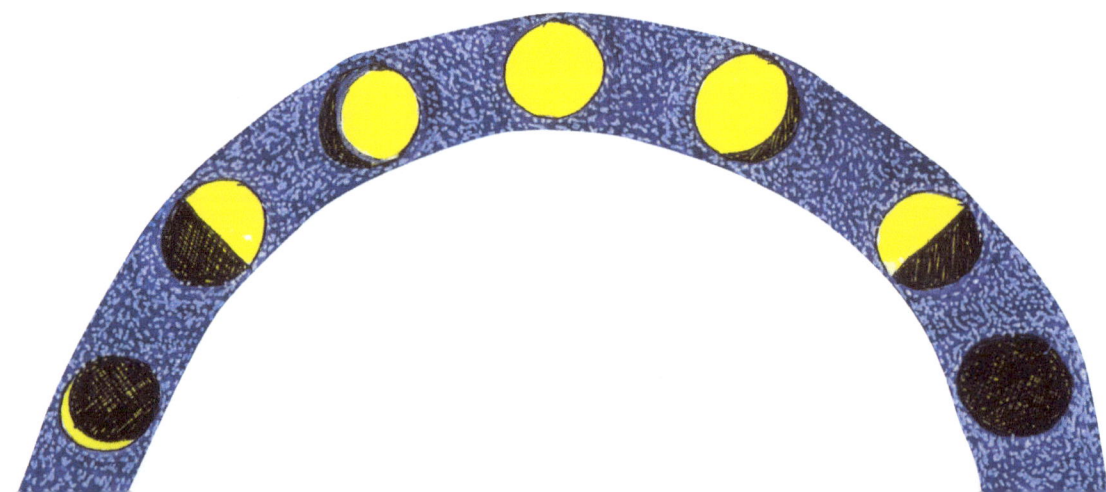

www.ingramcontent.com/pod-product-compliance
Lightning Source LLC
Chambersburg PA
CBHW060810090426
42736CB00003B/217